This book belongs to:

_____

A catalogue record for this book is available from the British Library

Published by Ladybird Books Ltd
80 Strand London WC2R 0RL
A Penguin Company

2 4 6 8 10 9 7 5 3 1
© LADYBIRD BOOKS LTD MMVIII
LADYBIRD and the device of a Ladybird are trademarks of Ladybird Books Ltd

ISBN: 978-1-84646-818-6

Printed in China

My best book about...

Baby Animals

Written by Stella Maidment
Illustrated by Katie Saunders

Look at all these baby animals!
Can you match them to their mothers?

A baby horse is called a foal.

Do you know what these babies are called?

Some animals have just one baby.
Can you help this mother bear
find her cub?

Some animals have lots of babies.
How many rabbits can you find?

What do all these different animals have in common?

Some animals walk soon after they are born. Where are these mothers and babies going?

Other baby animals need a little help to get around. How did you get around when you were a baby?

Some baby animals are tiny.
Some are bigger than you!
Which are big and which are small?

Where do these baby animals sleep?
Would you like to sleep there?

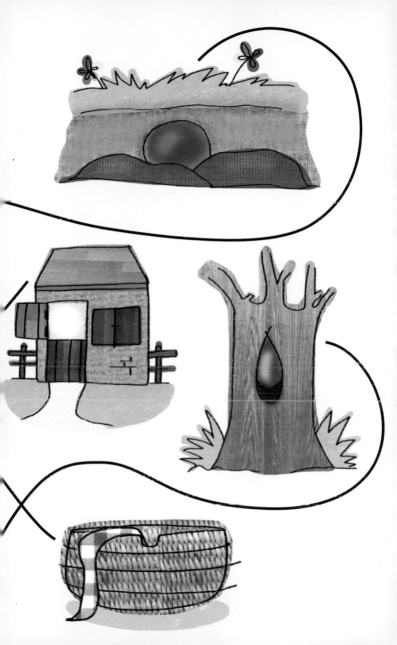

You can see baby animals on television.

Can you find five differences
between these two pictures?

You can see baby animals in wildlife parks and zoos.

Look at the pictures and say what is happening.

3)

4)

You might even have a baby animal at home!

If these were your pets, what would you name them?